© Aladdin Books Ltd 1998

Designed and produced by
Aladdin Books Ltd
28 Percy Street
London W1P 0LD

*First published in the United States
in 1998 by*
Copper Beech Books,
an imprint of
The Millbrook Press
2 Old New Milford Road
Brookfield, Connecticut 06804

Designed by
David West Children's Books
Computer illustrations
Stephen Sweet (Simon Girling & Associates)
Picture Research
Brooks Krikler Research
Project Editor
Sally Hewitt
Editors
Liz White/Sarah Levete

Printed in Belgium

Library of Congress Cataloging-in-Publication Data
Taylor, Helen (Helen Suzanne), 1963-
Plants feed on sunlight : and other facts about things that
grow / by Helen Taylor ; illustrated by Stephen Sweet.
p. cm. — (You'd never believe it but—)
Summary: Discusses plants, what they need to grow,
how and where they grow, and the many ways people
use them.
ISBN 0-7613-0814-8 (lib. bdg.)
1. Plants—Juvenile literature. 2. Growth (Plants)—Juvenile
literature. [1. Plants. 2. Growth (Plants)]
I. Sweet, Stephen, 1965- ill. II. Title. III. Series.
QK49.T39 1998
580—dc21   97-51778
                                           CIP AC

YOU'D *never* BELIEVE IT BUT...

plants feed on sunlight

and other facts about how things grow

Helen Taylor

COPPER BEECH BOOKS
BROOKFIELD, CONNECTICUT

Contents

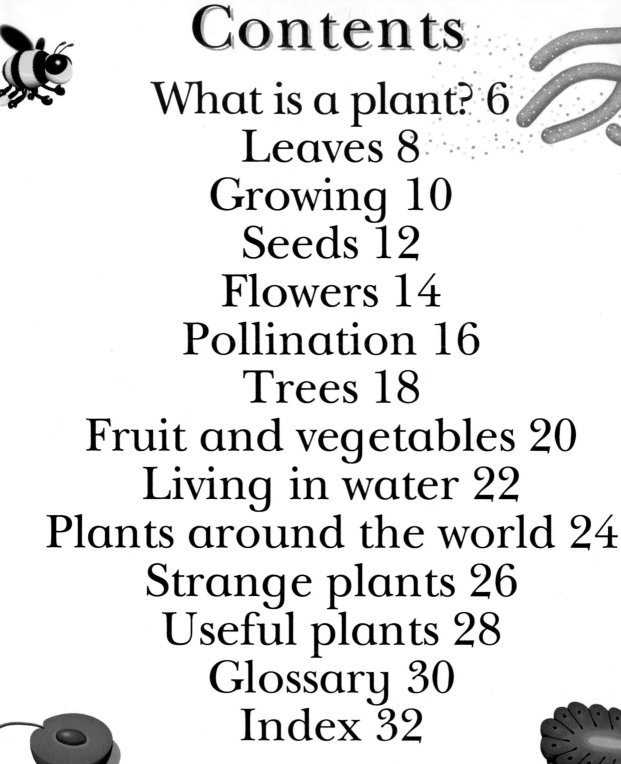

What is a plant? 6
Leaves 8
Growing 10
Seeds 12
Flowers 14
Pollination 16
Trees 18
Fruit and vegetables 20
Living in water 22
Plants around the world 24
Strange plants 26
Useful plants 28
Glossary 30
Index 32

Introduction

Seaweed floating underwater and daffodils nodding in the sunshine look very different, but they are both plants. There are thousands of different types of plants in the world. Plants are amazing — they provide us with much of our food as well as making their own food!

Join Jack and Jo as they discover all about plants, from how plants grow to how plants eat.

FUN PROJECTS Wherever you see this sign, it means there is a fun project that you can do. Each project will help you to understand more about the subject.

When you need to pick a plant for the project, make sure it is not a wild or rare plant.

What is a plant?

Plants are living things. Most plants make their own food from air, sunlight, and water. Without plants, people and animals could not survive. They provide food for us to eat. Plants give us oxygen for the air we breathe in and get rid of the carbon dioxide we breathe out.

Plants grow indoors and outdoors. They grow between rocks high up a mountain, in hot, dry deserts, and under the sea.

Is a great big tree a plant?

Yes. So is a tiny daisy.

Many plants grow flowers. All flowering plants have the same parts as this one.

Many flowers have colorful petals.

A strong stem holds the plant upright.

New leaves and flowers are tightly curled inside buds.

Green leaves collect sunlight to make food for the plant.

PLANT PARTS
Find some plants that have flowers. Which of these parts can you see?

Water and minerals that the plant needs to grow are sucked up from the soil by the roots.

You'd never believe it but...
Plants feed on sunlight! Plants don't need to go looking for food because they can make their own. They use energy from sunlight to make food in their green leaves.

Leaves

Plants use the green color in their leaves to make food from sunlight. Plants growing near a dark forest floor must have big leaves to catch as much sunlight as possible.

Water enters the plant's roots. It travels up the stem and into the leaves. Water helps the plant to grow.

This plant needs some water. Its leaves are droopy.

In very wet countries plants have shiny leaves to help the rain run off them.

Cactus plants have spines for leaves. These stop animals from eating them. Water is stored in the stem.

You'd never believe it but...

Plants sweat! They do this to get rid of any water that they don't need. Most leaves have tiny holes to let air in and water out.

Don't give it too much water. That will make the leaves droop too!

SWEATING PLANTS
1. Ask an adult to help you to tie a clear plastic bag around a house plant.
2. Leave it in a warm place. What happens to the bag?
3. Now, untie the bag.

Growing

If you look carefully at plants you will be able to see how they grow and change as the year goes by.

In the spring, when the weather starts to get warm, green shoots push up through the soil. Soon, the shoots will grow bigger and leaves will uncurl. Colorful flowers open in the sunshine. You can see insects buzzing around, collecting pollen from the flowers.

You'd never believe it but...

During the cold winter months, most plants stop growing and flowering. They are resting, waiting to grow again when the warmer spring weather arrives.

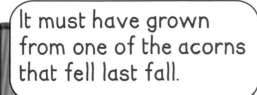

It must have grown from one of the acorns that fell last fall.

During the fall, flowers lose their petals. The part of the plant that holds the seeds, called the fruit, stays on the plant.

Cherry

Apple

Plum

Blackberry

Nuts, berries, and apples all hold seeds. They fall onto the ground. Soil and leaves cover them before they begin to grow.

Seeds

Most new plants grow from seeds. Each plant makes its own special kind of seed. Seeds have different ways of leaving the plant they came from to find somewhere to grow.

Seeds from the maple tree have wings to fly away from the tree.

I've collected all these seeds from the fruit I've eaten.

Birds eat berries with seeds inside them. The seeds land on the ground in bird droppings.

Dandelion seeds make fluffy parachutes that fly in the wind.

You'd never believe it but...

Some seeds, such as the Indian lotus, can grow even when they are a thousand years old. This picture shows the seed case of a lotus flower.

I wonder which ones will grow.

A new plant lives off the nutrients inside the seed. Later, when the leaves grow and make food for the plant, the seed shrivels up.

PLANTING SEEDS
1. Collect the pits, seeds, and stones from inside the fruit you eat.
2. Plant them in soil. Water them and see if they grow.

Flowers

The flower on a plant has a very important job to do. This is where the seeds are made. New plants grow from the seeds.

The dust on the stamens is called pollen. Pollen from a stamen is taken to a pistil so that new seeds can be made.

Pollen

Stamen

Petal

Pistil

Sepal

I've got some yellow pollen on my finger.

LOOK AT A FLOWER
1. Ask an adult which flower you can pick. Carefully pick off some of the petals. Look at the parts of the flower.
2. Now find a flower bud. Can you see that the sepals are closed to protect it?

Many flowers make a sugary juice called nectar that butterflies and other insects like to drink. Pollen rubs off onto the insects that land on the flower. They carry it onto the next flower they visit. Now, a new seed can be made.

> Don't get it in your nose. It might make you sneeze!

Catkins are a kind of flower. Wind blows pollen from one catkin to another.

You'd never believe it but...

The *Puya raymondii* plant, found in Bolivia, lives for over one hundred years before it grows just one huge flower.

After the flower has grown and seeds for a new plant have been made, the old plant dies.

Pollination

Bright colors and smells attract insects and birds to visit flowers so they can drink nectar and carry away pollen. Carrying pollen from flower to flower is called pollination.

Why does honeysuckle smell sweet in the evening?

So that moths can find it in the dark!

Moths and butterflies are attracted by sweet smells.

You'd never believe it but...

Some plants eat insects! A pitcher plant attracts flies that come looking for food but the plant eats them!

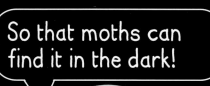

A bee orchid flower can fool a male bee into visiting it, by looking just like a female bee!

Most insects cannot see the color red, but birds can. This bright red flower attracts birds to drink its nectar. The birds carry pollen from flower to flower.

RAINBOW COLORS
Can you find a leaf or a petal from different plants for every color of the rainbow?

Trees

Trees start life as tiny seeds, but they grow into the tallest plants. They grow strong, woody stems called trunks so they can stay upright.

A tree makes a good home for all kinds of different creatures. Choose a tree near where you live. Keep a lookout for the creatures that visit it or live there.

There's a bird's nest in the branches.

I wonder if a squirrel lives in that hole.

You'd never believe it but...

The trunk of a giant redwood tree in California is so enormous that a car can drive through an arch cut into it.

Every year a tree grows a new layer around its trunk. If you look at a slice from a tree trunk you can see lots of rings. By counting the rings you can tell how old the tree is. Some trees are hundreds of years old.

BARK RUBBINGS

The bark of each kind of tree has a different pattern.
1. Take a piece of paper and put it against a tree trunk.
2. Rub it evenly with a wax crayon. What does the pattern look like? Now try a different tree.

Fruit and vegetables

Do you like eating fruit and vegetables? They are very good for you and they taste good, too. You can cook them in different ways, or you can eat fruit and most vegetables raw and crunchy.

When you eat vegetables it can be difficult to tell what part of the plant you are eating.

Root   Stalk   Leaves

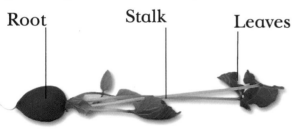

Radishes, turnips, and carrots are kinds of roots. They grow beneath the soil.

My celery looks like a stalk.

You'd never believe it but...

Potatoes have eyes! But they are not eyes to see with — they grow into new potato plants.

Is a tomato a fruit or a vegetable?

Take a good look at the vegetables next time you go shopping. Can you tell which part of the plant they come from?

VEGETABLE AND FRUIT PRINTS

1. Ask an adult to help you to cut some fruit or vegetables in half. Apples and potatoes work well.

2. Cut away some of the surface leaving a raised shape. Paint these in bright colors. With the paint still wet, press the shapes onto some paper.

Answer: A tomato is a fruit. A fruit is the part of the plant that contains the seeds.

Living in water

Many kinds of plants grow in ponds and streams. Some grow completely underwater. Plants make oxygen, which keeps the water fresh and clean.

Underwater plants have stems that can bend and feathery leaves that move with running water.

You should always have plants in a fish tank.

FLOATING OR SINKING?
1. Collect leaves of several different shapes and sizes.
2. Drop them in a bowl of water. Do they float or sink?

You'd never believe it but...

The leaves of the Amazonian water lily are so big that they can support a small child.

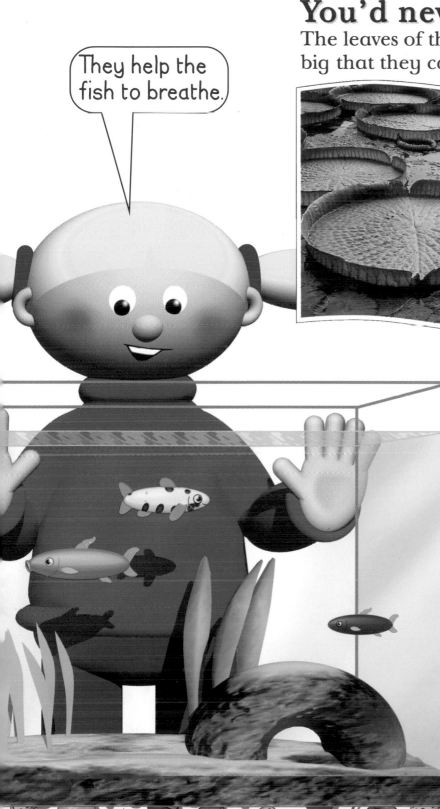

They help the fish to breathe.

Water lilies have flat, waterproof leaves called lily pads. They float on the water like little boats.

Plants around the world

Plants are very good at making the best of where they live. They will grow wherever they get the chance. Plants can do some amazing things!

Plants that live high in the mountains grow close to the ground. They have small leaves and flowers to keep out of the way of icy winds.

A weed has grown through the concrete!

It must be very strong.

You'd never believe it but...

Some desert plants look just like pebbles. This fools desert animals who like to eat plants.

Seeds lie under the hot desert sand waiting for rain. When it comes, they grow very quickly and burst into flower, like these poppy flowers. After a few days they die.

Giant rain forest trees grow very tall, as tall as an apartment building! Their tops can even touch the clouds. Young trees grow in the shade of the taller, older trees.

NO PLANTS AT ALL

Next time you go outside, see if you can stand somewhere where you can see no plants growing at all. It's very hard to do!

Strange plants

Some plants look very strange. Some plants that look strange are not really plants at all! They are called fungi.

A puffball is a fungus. It puffs out spores that are a little like seeds. These land and eventually grow into new puffballs.

> I've left this bread to go moldy!

> Did you know that mold is really a fungus?

> Ugh! I can't eat it now.

A tumbleweed is like a ball. It bounces and rolls along in the wind, spreading seeds as it goes.

You'd never believe it but...
A Venus fly trap snaps up flies — and eats them!

The largest flower in the world, the giant rafflesia, grows in the jungle. It has a terrible smell.

WEIRD AND WONDERFUL
Paint an imaginary plant. Does it have flowers and leaves? Where does it grow? How does it get its food? Give it a weird and wonderful name.

people-eating plant

Venus people trap

Leaves

Flowers

Root

Useful plants

Plants provide oxygen for the air we breathe. Much of our food comes from plants. Wooden furniture is made from tree trunks. Paper was once a tree, too. Can you find some more things that come from plants?

You'd never believe it but...

Most cars cannot run without using plants that are millions of years old!

Gasoline is made from oil that comes from tiny sea plants that were buried at the bottom of the ocean millions of years ago.

Do your shoes have rubber soles? Rubber is made from the liquid that flows out of the trunk of a rubber tree.

MAKE YOUR OWN ROPE
You can make a strong rope by braiding long grasses.
1. Make three pieces of grass into a braid. Pull it tightly.
2. Pull on the rope you have made. Which is stronger, your rope or one piece of grass?

Roots, stems, seeds, berries, leaves, and flowers of different plants are all used to make medicines. Oil from eucalyptus leaves is used in cough medicine.

The plant is called sisal.

This is made from a plant.

Glossary

Bark

Bark is the outside layer of a tree. It helps to protect the tree.

Bud

A bud is the part of a plant where new leaves and flowers are curled up before they are ready to open out.

Carbon dioxide

Carbon dioxide is a gas in the air. Animals breathe out carbon dioxide. Plants take in carbon dioxide, which helps them to make food.

Desert

A desert is a place where very little rain falls. The ground is rocky or sandy. Some deserts may be very hot, but deserts can be very cold, too.

Energy

All living things need energy to grow. People and animals get energy from food. Plants use sunlight to make food that gives them energy.

Flower

A flower is the part of a plant where seeds that will grow into new plants are made. Many flowers have colorful petals and a sweet smell to attract birds and insects.

Fruit

The fruit is the part of a plant that carries the new seeds it has made. An apple is the fruit of an apple tree. Apple pits are the seeds that will grow into new apple trees.

Leaf

A leaf grows on the stem of a plant. Plants use the green color in their leaves to make food from sunlight.

Nectar

Nectar is the sugary juice that plants make in their flowers. It attracts birds and insects so they will polinate the flower.

Oxygen

Oxygen is a gas in the air. People and animals need to breathe oxygen to survive. Plants give off oxygen into the air through their leaves.

Pollen

Pollen is made in flowers. It is the dust on the stamens that is carried to the pistils.

Pollination

Pollination takes place when pollen is transfered from one flower to another so that new seeds can be made.

Rain forest

A rain forest grows where it is warm and rain falls all year around.

Root

A root is the part of a plant that grows down into the soil to hold the plant in place. Roots soak up water and minerals that the plant needs to grow.

Seed

A new plant grows from a seed. A seed has a tough case for protection. It is packed with the food a new plant needs before it grows leaves and can make its own food.

Stem

A stem supports a plant. Leaves and flowers grow from the stem above the ground. Water travels up the stem.

Waterproof

Water cannot soak into things that are waterproof. Raindrops roll off thick, shiny waterproof leaves.

Index

B

bark 19, 30
birds 12, 16, 17, 18
buds 7, 30

C

carbon dioxide 6, 30
colors 16, 17, 21, 30

D

deserts 6, 24, 25, 30

E

energy 30

F

flowers 7, 10, 11, 13,
  14, 15, 16, 24, 25, 27, 30
food 5, 6, 7, 8, 13, 27, 28
fruit 11, 12, 13, 20, 21, 30

L

leaves 7, 8, 9, 10, 11,
  17, 20, 22, 23, 24, 27,
  29, 30

N

nectar 15, 16, 30

O

oxygen 6, 22, 28, 30

P

petals 7, 11, 14, 17, 30
pistils 14
pollen 10, 14, 15, 16, 30
pollination 16, 17, 30

R

rare plants 5
roots 7, 8, 20, 27, 29, 30

S

seeds 11, 12, 13, 14,
  15, 18, 25, 26, 29, 31
sepals 14
soil 7, 10, 11, 20
stamens 14, 31
stems 7, 8, 18, 22, 29, 30
sunlight 6, 7, 8, 30

T

trees 6, 10, 12, 18, 19,
  28, 29

V

vegetables 20, 21

W

water 7, 8, 9, 13, 22
waterproof 23, 31
wind 13, 15, 24, 26

PHOTO CREDITS

Abbreviations: t – top; m – middle; b – bottom;
r – right; l – left; c – center

All the pictures in this book were supplied by the Bruce
Coleman Collection apart from the following pages:
7, 13b, 15 all, 18-19, 21b, 22b, 26, & 27b — Roger
Vlitos; 14 — Spectrum Color Library.